Trying Weather

by Nancy Tyler
illustrated by Angela Adams

Practice Decodable 64

McGraw Hill Education

Bothell, WA • Chicago, IL • Columbus, OH • New York, NY

MHEonline.com

Send all inquiries to:
McGraw-Hill Education
8787 Orion Place
Columbus, OH 43240

ISBN: 978-0-02-145041-1
MHID: 0-02-145041-2

Printed in China.

8 9 10 11 12 DSS 27 26 25 24 23

Thursday was hot and dry.
Bright sun filled the sky.

"I will dress in my shorts," said Stella.
Then the day turned rainy and chilly.

"I am wet and cold!" Stella cried.
"Don't dress that way," said Mom.

Friday was dry, too.
But Stella did not try on shorts.

"I have on my rain jacket and sweater."
And I will tie on my hat."

Friday stayed dry, but Stella did not.
"I am wet with sweat," she cried.